Witness Lee

The Practice of the Group Meetings

Living Stream Ministry
Anaheim, CA • www.lsm.org

First Edition, November 1990.

ISBN 978-0-87083-551-3

Published by

Living Stream Ministry
2431 W. La Palma Ave., Anaheim, CA 92801 U.S.A.
P. O. Box 2121, Anaheim, CA 92814 U.S.A.

Printed in the United States of America

12 13 14 15 16 / 9 8 7 6 5 4 3

CONTENTS

PREFACE

This book is composed of messages given by Brother Witness Lee from February through May of 1990 in a full-time training in Anaheim, California.

CHAPTER ONE

PRACTICAL FELLOWSHIP CONCERNING THE GROUP MEETINGS

Scripture Reading: Heb. 10:24-25

In our study over the past five years, the Lord has shown us His ordained way for meeting and serving in the church. The God-ordained way comprises four steps: gospel preaching; the home meetings for feeding the young ones; the group meetings for shepherding, teaching, and perfecting the saints that they may be able to carry out the work of the New Testament ministry, that is, the building up of the Body of Christ; and prophesying in the church meetings. However, we have not yet found the practical way to carry out each of these steps. Our study of how to carry out door-knocking for the preaching of the gospel is not yet complete. There are very many ways to visit people by knocking on their doors, and we are still not satisfied with our present way. Likewise, we also need more study on how to feed our spiritual children in the home meetings. We know what the God-ordained way to meet and to serve is, but we do not know how to carry out that way. Therefore, we need more study.

THE NEED FOR MORE STUDY CONCERNING OUR WAY

An article in a recent newspaper reported that the Mormons have had a great success in knocking on people's doors. They have had a good increase especially among the ethnic minority groups. In Orange County in 1980 the Mormons had only about eight hundred members from the different minority groups. Today, however, their membership in the minority groups in Orange County comprises over four thousand. They have had a five-fold increase in less than ten years. In contrast to this, the number of saints in our Chinese-speaking meetings has barely doubled since 1983. The Mormons teach one of the greatest heresies in Christianity, but they have learned the proper way to do things. In Taiwan, they have even picked up some of the terminology we use in the Lord's recovery. They study their situations and always try to find a better way. When they go to visit Korean or Vietnamese homes, they send two Caucasians who can speak Korean or Vietnamese fluently. However, we have sent the saints out loosely. Those among us who go to visit Korean homes may not be able to speak any Korean. We trust blindly that the people in those homes can speak English, but some of them cannot. Our practice may be compared to asking a brother who has never had piano lessons to play the piano for us. This is the unlearned way. We have not learned the adequate way to carry out the God-ordained way.

The Mormon teaching is one of the greatest heresies, yet no one can deny that they have had a great success in the last century. They do not carry out their way loosely. The total number of missionaries sent out by the denominations is just over 50,000. The Mormons, however, have 40,000 missionaries in the foreign fields. Moreover, these young men have been restricted, balanced, trained, corrected, and adjusted. They are very punctual, faithful, and well-behaved. In some airports there are often two young, well-dressed Mormons. They may be Caucasian, but when a Chinese person gets off an airplane, they greet him in proper Mandarin and ask him if he needs a ride. They then take the Chinese person to his destination while they continue to speak with him. They try to learn what the person's needs are, and they offer to help him. Even the quality of their Mandarin speech draws admiration from others.

We have not practiced the proper way because we have not had the adequate learning. We know what the God-ordained way is, but we do not have the way to carry it out. When we go to middle-class Caucasian families, we may practice to send brothers who do not speak English properly or speak with an accent. These brothers will not be properly received by those families. If we would instead send three well-dressed brothers who speak properly, the middle-class families would not refuse to open their doors to them. Some have said that visiting people for the gospel by knocking on their doors does not work, at least not in America. We should not blame God's ordained way and say that it does not work. Rather, it is our way of carrying it out that does not work. Even the Son of God came into the world to visit people where they were, and He sent the twelve (Matt. 10:1, 5-6) and then the seventy (Luke 10:1) to visit others. This is God's way, but we must learn the proper way to carry it out. We have not yet seen the real issue of the God-ordained way because our way to carry it out is not satisfactory. This is why we have concluded that we need more study.

Some have said that to build up the church we do not need the work. They claim that we need only a proper living as a testimony. However, Paul not only worked, but he labored (Col. 1:29a), struggled (Col. 1:29b), and strived (Phil. 1:27). *Struggle* and *strive* are expressions used in relation to athletics. The Greek word for *struggle* can also be translated *wrestle*. In his work Paul considered himself an Olympic athlete. The New Testament also likens Christians to farmers (2 Tim. 2:6). A farmer who is lazy or who does not know how to farm cannot be successful. Farmers must learn much. They must learn about the seasons and the weather. They also must work diligently day and night. They must have the way, and they must also have diligence and wisdom.

We have been too loose in our way. The old way of Christianity not only annuls the function of the members of the Body of Christ but also makes everyone lazy. In the denominations it is sufficient to go to a meeting and leave an offering. A preacher is hired to work for the members. However, this is not the way of the Body of Christ. The Body of Christ does not hire anyone. Rather, it should stir up everyone to learn the way to meet and to serve.

THE GROUP MEETINGS

In the old way of meeting, we came together in the meeting hall to listen to a brother who was knowledgeable in the Bible. Since then we may have divided the large meeting into several group meetings. However, in these group meetings some of the new ones may ask questions that we are not able to answer. If we are not able to answer the new ones' questions in a practical way, this indicates that we do not know how to meet in the group meetings. We know that we should not return to the old way of meeting, so we may eventually compromise by inviting a knowledgeable brother to come to our group meeting to take care of its needs. This brother then becomes the Bible teacher, the "pastor," of the group meeting. On the one hand, we do have the group meetings, but on the other hand, we may still be in the old way. Although we may no longer meet under one roof but in several homes, we may still not be in the new way. We may appear to be in the new way but may still be practicing the old way.

To carry out the group meetings we need to learn how to have a practical fellowship, a mutual prayer, the care for one another, and the shepherding of the young ones. The first thing we need to care for is a practical fellowship among the attendants related to their daily life. The fellowship in the small groups should include such practical matters as the health and circumstances of the saints in the group. All the matters related to the practical life of all the persons meeting in the group should be covered in the fellowship. This kind of fellowship will spontaneously issue in prayer. According to the need, we can intercede for each other. This prayer need not be after the fellowship is over but should be mingled with the fellowship.

Then, we must practically care for the saints. We should not merely pray in spiritual terms; we must also be sent by the Lord to the needy ones. If we pray that the Lord would do something, we may be sent by Him to do it. The Lord is omnipotent, but if we do not do something practically to help the brother or sister for whom we pray, our prayer may not be answered. We may pray that the Lord meet the need of a brother who is in need of money, but the Lord may tell us that we must first meet his need from our own resources. The New Testament tells us that we need to love in practicality and not merely in word (1 John 3:16-18). We must have practical fellowship with practical prayer and practical care. Following this, some can go to visit the person for whom they have prayed. We must go to visit those who are in any suffering and participate in their suffering. This is to shepherd one another.

Our group meetings should be like this every time. This will attract people. Regardless of how strong, rich, or knowledgeable one is, he still desires help from others. Some saints feel lonely but are afraid to seek out fellowship with stronger ones. It is in the group meeting that we can render an adequate, sufficient care for the saints. It is in the group meeting that every saint's current situation can be made known. All the attendants of a proper group meeting will be built up together. This is the practical building up of the Body of Christ. Without the group meetings, we may talk about building up but never experience it.

The practical fellowship, prayer, care, and shepherding are the basic factors of the group meetings. If we do not practice these, we will have no way to take care of every saint's need. It would take twenty honest, diligent, knowledgeable, and capable elders to shepherd a church of two hundred saints. If they went out every day to visit and shepherd the saints, the church would be very strong. However, it is not practical to have this many full-time elders. Moreover, to care for the saints in this way is against the principle of the Body. The Body consists of all the members, and the members take care of the Body. We cannot hire others to take care of the Body. Every member should share in the care of the Body.

Hebrews 10:25 says, "Not forsaking the assembling of ourselves together, as the custom with some is, but exhorting one another, and so much the more as you see the day drawing near." The phrase "the assembling of ourselves together" indicates that the meeting spoken of in this verse is "our" meeting. We should not forsake the group meetings, which are our meetings. The small group meetings are the meetings of the members of the Body. Without a proper practice of the group meetings, it is not possible to care for and shepherd all the saints.

TEACHING IN THE GROUP MEETINGS BY ASKING AND ANSWERING QUESTIONS

In human society the way to teach people is to gather them

together as students with a single teacher. The traditional way of meeting in Christianity is also for a number of people to come together with a Bible teacher. However, Hebrews 10:24-25 says, "And let us consider one another for inciting to love and good works, not forsaking the assembling of ourselves together, as the custom with some is, but exhorting one another, and so much the more as you see the day drawing near." The phrases "consider one another," "inciting to love and good works," and "exhorting one another" indicate that the meeting spoken of in these verses is not a meeting for one to teach and the others to listen. This is a meeting in which all the attendants are the same, inciting and exhorting each other.

Ephesians 4:11-12 says, "And He gave some apostles, and some prophets, and some evangelists, and some shepherds and teachers, for the perfecting of the saints unto the work of ministry, unto the building up of the Body of Christ." All four categories of gifted persons perfect the saints. The evangelist may have a burden to perfect the saints in the matter of gospel preaching, to stir them up and teach the truths concerning the gospel. According to the natural way of thinking, he will ask the elders to arrange a meeting for this purpose once a week. Then each category of gifted ones will in turn arrange their own special meetings for perfecting the saints. This is not the way in which the gifted ones should perfect the saints. Rather, in a group meeting an apostle may be present, and there may also be a prophet, an evangelist, or a shepherd and teacher. Then spontaneously each one can teach in a mutual way.

In our study and experimentation, we have found that the best way to teach is to raise questions in the group meetings. By asking the proper questions and answering the questions of others, we spontaneously teach, instruct, and perfect others. In the past we prepared two sets of lesson books, *Truth Lessons* and *Life Lessons,* intending that they could be used in the home meetings and group meetings. When we prepared those lessons, we were not clear that the best way to teach mutually is to ask questions. We need to learn not only how to answer the questions of the new ones in the group meetings, but also how to ask questions. To ask questions in a proper way is even more difficult than to answer them. If we have a burden to teach a certain item, we should not teach it directly but turn this burden into a question. We may have a burden to teach the new ones about dealing with idols. However, we should not do this as a teacher. We should rather ask the saints in the group meeting how to deal with idols. This will stir up all the attendants to say something. There will be different kinds of answers with different points. Each one will say something, and all the speaking will become part of the teaching. Then a brother who knows more than the others can add something, and someone else can add even more. The result will be a very good and complete teaching concerning dealing with idols. This way of teaching by asking questions is not carried out by only one person. Rather, it gives an opportunity to all the attendants in the group meeting to function. Regardless of how much one knows and how good his speaking may be, one person's speaking can never compare with many answers.

By attending a group meeting like this every week for one or two years, the attendants will learn much. One week someone may ask how to deal with idols. Another week someone may ask how to pray. There is no systematized way and no fixed line of subjects. Whether the persons in the meeting have been saved for twenty years or two months, they all have some experience, and they all can say something. After attending group meetings in this way for three or four years, the saints will be perfected. This is not too long to wait. A child cannot be raised overnight. He must attend elementary school for six years, junior high school for two or three years, high school for three or four years, and then college for four more years. Then, after sixteen years of education, a young person is perfected and can go out to do something in society. This is the right way to perfect others, and we must learn to take this way. We cannot accomplish anything quickly. Some churches have been established for nearly sixteen years, but because we did not practice the proper way, they have not gained much. This can be compared to allowing our children to play and fight for sixteen years without ever sending them to school. After many years they will not have an education and will not be useful. This may be our situation. We may have wasted much time. From now on we need a change in our way. To build up a society we need the begetting, feeding, teaching, and building up of the children. The church is the heavenly, spiritual society. Thus, to build up the church, we need begetting in order to gain persons for the Lord. Then we need to feed those whom we have gained, and we must also teach them and build them up.

RAISING UP GROUP MEETINGS IN THE NEW WAY

The group meetings should be eighty percent of the church life. If we do not build up the group meetings, the church will be very weak. Among us there are some older saints who love the Lord and the church but do not have the habit of attending the group meetings. They have the habit only of coming to the Lord's table meeting, the ministry meeting, and sometimes the prayer meeting. Some may come only to take the Lord's table on the Lord's Day and leave an offering in the offering box. To charge, encourage, and exhort them to come to the group meetings will not work since they do not have such a habit. However, some of the older saints do have the burden to come to the group meetings. Many of them, though, have been in the traditional, old way for years. Their traditional way of meeting may be compared to speaking English with a foreign accent. Because of my old, traditional background, my English is somewhat poor. It is difficult for me to get rid of my old way of speaking. Likewise, it is difficult to drop the traditional way of meeting.

These older saints with the traditional ways will eventually be in the same group meetings as the newly baptized ones. The way to build up the group meetings, therefore, is first by going out to gain new ones. It is best not to raise up a group meeting with the older saints as the foundation. We should first go to gain new believers. After one or two new ones are gained, we should go to their home to feed them in their home meeting. This home meeting will become a group meeting. Then we may invite some older saints to join us. In this way we will have a mixed attendance with some new ones and some older ones.

We must let the new ones know that we do not care as much for the big meetings as we care for the group meetings. The group meetings are the "lifeline," the "pulse," of our church life. At the same time we should have a thorough fellowship with the older saints in the group, either in our home or in their home. We can tell them that they should forget about the old way of meeting and that they need to pick up the new way. In the first few group meetings, we need to explain what the new way is and how to have a group meeting. We should explain that we come together not in formality, but in a released spirit to fellowship, pray, care for one another, and shepherd one another.

Even though our current group meetings may have the element of oldness, we should not dissolve them. This will not be good for the attendants in those meetings. We still need to maintain the present meetings, but at the same time we should form a group in the new way. Our time and energy should be concentrated on the new group meeting. If some saints would raise up group meetings in the new way, after a few months many others will follow them to do the same. At that time the meetings in the older way will fade away by themselves.

We should not depend upon the church to arrange a group meeting for us. If we want a family, we should simply get married and bring forth children. We do not need to wait for our parents to arrange a family for us. An arranged family is not a genuine family. We need to produce the group meetings ourselves. Then we must learn the new way to have the group meetings. It is not sufficient to maintain a number of home meetings with only two or three members present. These smaller meetings will not be as effective as the group meetings and will not last for the long term. We need to go along with the need of the new ones, but in going along with their need, we must bring them into the new way. Then a proper, genuine group meeting will be built up with them. A group meeting formed and built up in a proper, spiritual way will endure for the long term. The church life depends upon this kind of group meeting. We need to learn the best way to have the group meetings, and we need to spend time to labor according to what we have learned.

CHAPTER TWO

BEING LIVING FOR THE GROUP MEETINGS

Scripture Reading: Heb. 10:24-25

THE GROUP MEETINGS

Hebrews 10:24-25 says, "And let us consider one another for inciting to love and good works, not forsaking the assembling of ourselves together, as the custom with some is, but exhorting one another, and so much the more as you see the day drawing near." The more we study these two verses, the more we can realize that they refer to the group meetings. The meetings spoken of here are meetings in mutuality. Verse 24 speaks of "inciting to love and good works," and verse 25 mentions "exhorting one another." Verse 25 tells us not to forsake the meetings—not the meetings in a general sense but in the sense of "the assembling of ourselves together." This indicates that as Christians we should have "our own" meeting. Before the Hebrew readers of this Epistle were saved, they had the Jewish way of meeting. Now as Christians they needed to have a Christian meeting, which they should have considered as "their" meeting. As Christians we should take care of the Christian meeting, which these verses call "the assembling of ourselves together."

In the church we have different kinds of meetings. We have a meeting on the Lord's Day. The Lord's Day meeting is not the same as the Sunday morning service in Christianity, but we do take advantage of the fact that the Lord's Day is a holiday in most nations. However, *Sunday* is not the Christian word for this day. *Sunday* is a term of idolatry, referring to the worship of the sun. To us, this day is the Lord's Day, and on this day we have a meeting. On Tuesday we may have a prayer meeting, and on Wednesday we may have a midweek meeting. Besides these, we have the group meetings. Among these four kinds of meetings, we should consider that the group meeting is our own meeting. The number who attend the group meetings should be higher than the number who attend the other kinds of meetings. Most brothers and sisters attend the Lord's Day morning meetings because most of them came from a traditional background. According to this background, "Sunday" is the time for Christians to worship God. If one does not come to the Sunday morning meeting, he is not regarded as a faithful Christian. However, the group meetings should be eighty percent of our church life. If in a local church the attendance in the Lord's Day morning meeting is higher than that in the group meetings, the saints in that church are still religious and in their traditional way. When in a local church the attendance in the group meetings is higher than that in the church meetings on the Lord's Day, that church is in the proper way. Whether a local church is in the proper way or not depends in part on the attendance in the group meetings.

MEETING IN SMALL GROUPS IN MUTUALITY

The Gospels and Acts speak of different kinds of meetings. Matthew 18:20 says, "For where two or three are gathered together in My name, there I am in their midst." According to verse 19, this is not a meeting in mutuality but a meeting for prayer with a particular burden. In Acts 12 there was such a meeting in the house of Mary, the mother of John Mark (v. 12). A number were assembled together to pray for Peter's release from prison. This was not a group meeting in mutuality for inciting and exhorting.

Before the day of Pentecost, there were only one hundred twenty Christians meeting together. They had been with the Lord for as long as three and a half years. Probably most of them had followed Jesus from Galilee. They had traveled with the Lord and seen His human living. Some of them had seen how He was arrested and judged, and a number of them had seen how He was nailed on the cross and how He hung there for six hours. They saw how the Lord was buried, and eventually they also saw how He was resurrected. They were with the Lord for forty days, from the day of the Lord's resurrection to the day of His ascension, enjoying His appearing and His hidden presence. Finally, they saw the Lord Jesus ascend to the third heavens. The one hundred twenty had received an excellent view of the Lord. This made them bold and even beside themselves. After the Lord's ascension, they returned to Jerusalem and prayed in one accord for ten days to be clothed with power from on high. On the day of Pentecost they received the outpouring of the Spirit, and they began to preach and to propagate Christ.

Acts 2:46 says, "And day by day, continuing steadfastly with one accord in the temple and breaking bread from house to house, they took their food with exultation and simplicity of heart." Acts 5:42 says, "And every day, in the temple and from house to house, they did not cease teaching and bringing the good news of Jesus as the Christ." These verses tell us that the Christians met in their homes, and the number of home meetings was according to the number of homes. They met in this way for preaching Christ, teaching, breaking bread, prayer, and fellowship. However, there is no indication of the way they preached and taught. In principle, it must have been in the way of mutuality.

On the day of Pentecost, three thousand people were saved and baptized. It is helpful to consider how three thousand people could have been baptized on the same day. The homes of that time had a pool which was used for bathing. Acts 16:31-34 tells us how Paul and Silas preached the gospel to the Philippian jailer and his household. Verses 33b-34a say, "And he was baptized immediately, he and all his household. And he brought them up into his house and set a table before them." The phrase "he brought them up" indicates that the jailer and his household were baptized probably in the bathing pool in the lower part of the house. On the day of Pentecost, the three thousand were probably baptized in the homes of the believers. Moreover, the baptisms were probably not carried out by a few persons only, such as Peter and John, but by many persons. In the Gospels, when the Lord Jesus fed the five thousand, He told the disciples to make the people sit down in groups (Mark 6:39-40; Luke 9:14). The disciples must have learned this way from the Lord. On the day of Pentecost, when three thousand people were to be baptized, the disciples probably divided them into groups. In this way the one hundred twenty could baptize three thousand persons in less than a day.

From that time the believers continued to meet in their homes by groups (Acts 2:42, 46). Acts 5:42 says that in the homes "they did not cease teaching and bringing the good news of Jesus as the Christ." We may ask how there could have been enough teachers for all the home meetings. According to the principle in the New Testament (1 Cor. 14:26), it is doubtful that only one person in each group taught and all the others listened. The newly saved and baptized ones, being full of the Lord, must have had something with which to bubble over. They all could have said something regarding their salvation. It is doubtful that all of the many new believers were dumb, waiting for Peter or John to say something. Peter and John could not have been in every group meeting. The first meetings of the church must have been "bubbling" meetings. Everyone there must have been beside himself.

"BUBBLING" AND BEING BESIDE OURSELVES IN THE GROUP MEETINGS

Group meetings in which the saints "bubble" are the proper church meetings and the proper church life. A group meeting is a meeting full of mutuality. In such a meeting everyone speaks and everyone "bubbles." Such meetings are full of activity. It is doubtful that the meetings of the thousands of new believers on the day of Pentecost kept a certain sequence, with a particular brother praying, another brother calling a hymn, and a designated brother reading the Scriptures. They simply "bubbled," sang, and testified in their group meetings.

Many times if no one instructs the saints to begin to read the Bible, to pray, or to sing, no one will do it. We should not need to be instructed as to what to do in the meetings. We are living persons. We should come singing and praising. However, in many of today's meetings, if no one says, "Let us read the Bible," no one opens the Bible. That kind of meeting is still very much in the traditional way of religion. Many times our reading of the Bible in the meetings is done in a set way. It is of the flesh to do something with the purpose of being different from religion, but we do not need to be the same every time. If a certain verse is wonderful to us, we can read it in a living way. If in a long list of verses we find Hebrews 10:24-25, we can say, "Hallelujah for Hebrews 10:24-25!" and read it before we read the other verses. Then when we come to the phrase "inciting to love and good works," we can say, "Oh, inciting! We need to incite one another!"

Our old way of meeting can be seen in the big meetings as well as in the group meetings. In a recent conference meeting there were seventeen hundred attendants, but the meeting still kept a fixed sequence. When the saints began coming together, no one declared the banners, read the Scripture references, or called a hymn. Sometimes most of the attendants in a meeting are quiet. This quietness is like the dumbness of idols (1 Cor. 12:2). Some may say that to shout "Hallelujah!" in the meetings is not the proper worship of God. However, God would rather that we be beside ourselves in the meetings than worship in a dead way.

The quiet way of meeting is the tradition of religion. Traditional Christianity has influenced us to meet in this way. Before we were saved, we already knew how to worship God in the traditional way. Even a Moslem knows how to meet in a "Christian" way. If a Moslem becomes a Christian, he will feel that he already knows the way he should worship as a Christian. However, the many new believers on the day of Pentecost had no idea how to meet. They knew how to meet in the Jewish way, but on that day they saw something that caused them to be beside themselves. They no longer cared for the Jewish things. Therefore, they met in their meetings in a "bubbling" way. Our meetings should be full of shouting, praising, singing, and speaking in a "bubbling" way. This is the way for Christians to meet. When we bring new believers to this kind of meeting, they will receive a proper impression of the way to meet, and they will never forget that impression.

PRAYING, CONFESSING, AND NOT QUENCHING THE SPIRIT

Young children do not need to be introduced and formally organized in order to play together. If they are simply put together for a few minutes, they will mingle together and become a lively group. Living children play well together. Even if you charge them not to play too actively, they will still do it because they are so living. When we go to the group meetings, we also should be living. We should not go in oldness. If we are dead and stale, we lose our capacity to have a proper group meeting. We were regenerated years ago, but now we need to be transformed and renewed. We need to get out of the old habit, thought, concept, and logic. We need to get out of the old Christianity. The only way to do this is to pray. We should not pray superficially but from our spirit. When we pray, we should also make a thorough confession of all our failures, defects, shortcomings, wrongdoings, mistakes, and transgressions. We should confess our criticizing of others, our backbiting, gossiping, and vain, idle words. Our confessing should not be once for all. We need to confess every day, several times a day. In this way we will pray ourselves into our spirit. We will be happy, rejoicing, and joyful the whole day. We will be persons filled with the Spirit and possessed by the Spirit. We will become different persons. We should not speak negatively but always speak positively. We should no longer gossip, criticize, or speak idly. We should simply speak Christ, speak grace, speak mercy, speak God, and speak the holy Word. This will change the very essence of our being. We need such a change. I hope we would all live in this way.

Living in this way will cause us to be Christians who meet all the time. Even when we are not in a meeting, we will be joyful and rejoicing persons. Then when we come together with others, we will still be this way. We will be very willing to open ourselves and fellowship. We will be able to present to the saints what we have, what we are, and what we know. When we come together with others, we will take the lead to be such a person. Then the others, especially the new ones, will follow us.

We should come together with six to eight brothers or

sisters to practice this kind of group meeting. If we are not able to have this kind of meeting with one another, then we will not be able to do it with the new ones. Instead of taking the lead to be living, we may take the lead to be dumb. After five minutes of dumbness we may say, "Let us open up to fellowship," but no one would fellowship. This kind of meeting is dumb, calm, and cold. There is no warmth, no spirit, and no life. In such a meeting the Spirit is quenched. First Thessalonians 5:19 says, "Do not quench the Spirit." We quench the Holy Spirit by quenching our human spirit. Sometimes when everyone is singing "Hallelujah!" in the meeting, we do not join in, or we sing in a cold way. This quenches our spirit. We need to join in and open up. Then our spirit will be stirred up. When our human spirit is stirred up, the Holy Spirit within us rises up, and we receive the benefit. We must learn not to quench our spirit.

Our spirit is our most tender part and our most excitable part. No other part of our being can be excited in a proper way as our spirit. Every spiritual person must be able to be beside himself in his spirit. If we are too composed, we cannot be spiritual. The Apostle Paul knew how to weep (Rom. 12:15; Phil. 3:18) and, at the proper time, how to be joyful (Phil. 4:4). A person who is too sober-minded never laughs and never weeps. It is difficult for the brothers to be spiritual, because they control themselves too much. The sisters, however, do not control themselves as much. In this sense it is easier for them to be spiritual. In the four Gospels women such as Mary Magdalene, Joanna, and Susanna (Luke 8:2-3) were all spiritual. Judas, on the other hand, had a very clear, sober mind, a mind that considered how much money he could gain by betraying the Lord. We must learn not to quench our spirit, and we must learn to release our spirit. We should all learn to be "females." Then we will have the capacity to have proper group meetings.

Chapter Three

RAISING UP THE BELIEVERS IN THE GROUP MEETINGS

BEGETTING AND RAISING NEW BELIEVERS

The way for the church to practice the God-ordained way to meet and to serve is first through the exercise of the New Testament priesthood of the gospel by preaching the gospel through visiting people. We must first bring people to be regenerated and baptized. This is to produce new believers by begetting them. Then we need to raise up group meetings to build up the new ones, to perfect them, and to raise them up. To raise the new believers is harder than to beget them. All parents know that begetting a child is easy. After the delivery of a child, a mother must feed her child several times a day. Although this can be troublesome, it is not difficult. However, to raise a child for over twenty years is not easy. After being fed, a child begins to grow. Eventually, the child must be sent to kindergarten. Later, he must be sent to elementary school, junior high school, and high school. At home also the parents must do many things. They must instruct, correct, and discipline the child. They must also provide food, clothing, lodging, and many other items. Much has to be done in order to properly raise the child. After more than twenty years, the child will graduate from college. Then he will be useful, not just for making a living but for doing things that can help his society. Raising the new believers is the purpose of the group meetings.

Acts 20 reveals Paul's heart and practice regarding the raising up of the believers. He called for the elders from Ephesus to meet with him in Miletus, and he told them, "Wherefore watch, remembering that for three years, night and day, I did not cease admonishing each one with tears" (v. 31). He said, "I did not shrink from declaring to you anything that was profitable, and to teach you publicly and from house to house" (v. 20). Paul exhorted and admonished the believers, both publicly in the big meetings and privately from house to house. He did not shrink from telling them of all the things they needed to live their daily life according to the will of God. He told them all the things concerning God's counsel, the mysteries of God's economy, and he told them how to fulfill God's eternal plan concerning the mystery of God, Christ (Col. 2:2), and the mystery of Christ, the church (Eph. 3:4, 9-10). Raising up the new believers in the way Paul did cannot be accomplished merely by the big meetings of the church. Even the home meetings for feeding the believers are not adequate to raise them up in this way. To raise up the believers in this way requires the group meetings.

If only a few saints know the proper way to preach the gospel and have group meetings, they will be able to go anywhere and raise up new believers within a short time. They will be desperate to get a few people saved and will then teach them in the way Paul did. These new believers, who formerly might have been heathens who knew nothing about Christianity, will have a very good group meeting within a few months. Many of us, however, came from the background of traditional Christianity, and it is not easy to change our way. Even if we practice the group meetings, we may not do it in the new way. Our oldness and staleness damages our practice of the group meetings. We need a change of mind. We all are able to change, but whether or not we change depends upon our desperation. We must not merely receive the speaking in these messages and appreciate and agree with all the points. We must be desperate to have a radical change. Without this desperation we will still have group meetings with spiritually old saints in the old way with the old concept. This is not effective. We must be stirred up to have a change. We desperately need a new start and new group meetings.

OUR NEED FOR COACHING AND LEARNING

It has been good that we have had group meetings in the

past. They accomplished something. However, we can always find a better way in anything we do. This is why we need a coach to help us to "play ball." If we have never been coached, we will not have the proper way. Our group meetings of the past were better than nothing, but we must realize that they might not have been carried out in the coached way. We need coaching. We should not "play ball" in any way we desire. If we are coached, we will learn how to "play" properly, and we will be successful.

Paul received the revelation of God's economy, which he revealed in his Epistles (Eph. 3:3, 9). We, however, were not born nineteen centuries ago, and we did not receive the revelation directly from the Lord as Paul did. Nevertheless, we have a better heritage than Paul had. Paul did not have nineteen centuries of church history to study, but we have studied church history very much, not just to learn the facts of history, but mainly to discover what the best way for the church is. We have tried to learn which ways worked and which ways did not work. During the past five years, we spent much time to reconsider all the practices of Christianity over the last twenty years. We tried to learn what God's ordained way is and what the biblical way to preach the gospel is. We studied and restudied the Bible, and we eventually discovered from Paul's writings the truth of the New Testament priesthood of the gospel. Every preacher of the New Testament gospel must be not an ordinary person but a priest. Then we compared this truth to the practices of gospel preaching in the Catholic Church, the state churches, and the denominations. We considered how the Brethren, the Pentecostals, and the free groups preach the gospel. We also studied how we preached the gospel in the past. Now we have learned that the top way, God's ordained, biblical way, is the way we are passing on in these messages.

TAKING THE NEW WAY WITH DESPERATION

The "new way" is the God-ordained way and the biblical way. The church has been on the earth for almost twenty centuries. I have the full assurance and confidence that now is the time for the Lord to carry out His new way. The carrying out of the new way can be compared to the tide of democracy on the earth today. The political history of the past six thousand years has consummated in democracy, and now the eastern European countries, the former Russian satellites, have turned from autocracy to democracy. The carrying out of the Lord's way, also, is like the coming of a tide. The God-ordained way to meet and to serve is recorded in the Bible, and every word spoken by the Lord will be fulfilled (Matt. 5:18; 24:35). His words were not spoken in vain (Isa. 55:10-11). Therefore, we must learn to take this way. If we mean business with the Lord, we must make a decision to have a radical change in our understanding concerning the Lord's way.

The problem among us is that we have become old and stale, and we have not adopted the new way with desperation. If we will be desperate, we will have a success. Our lack of desperation can be seen in the way we visit people. In the past we have gone to visit people too lightly and without adequate preparation. Even in the matter of speaking the language of those we contact, we have not been adequately prepared. Those who visit a Korean-speaking family should be able to speak Korean. We have been too loose in choosing whom we send to contact certain persons. If we send brothers from ethnic minorities to visit a middle-class Caucasian family, they may not be properly received. The family may be cold toward them. On the other hand, if four middle-aged Caucasian brothers and sisters visit the same family, they will not be rejected. The doors and hearts of that family will be opened. Likewise, if we want to gain a Japanese family, we should send Japanese brothers and sisters to visit them. We have not considered these matters thoroughly. We have acted too lightly. We must mean business with the Lord or we will waste our time.

We need to reconsider our ways. We have practiced the old way for many years, and it was not effective. This should compel us to take the new way. We have no choice but to take this way. To take the new way is not difficult. We must simply pick it up and make the decision to go on according to it. According to our study and experience, we must first go to beget new believers. Within two or three weeks we can beget two or three new ones. Then we should form a new group meeting with these new persons, and we must strictly practice the new group meeting according to the way in which we were coached. Then we should continue to make improvements when possible. We should try our best to follow this way.

CHAPTER FOUR

BEING RELEASED, LIVING, AND FRESH FOR THE GROUP MEETINGS

THE CARRYING OUT OF THE GOD-ORDAINED WAY TO MEET AND TO SERVE

The first step in the carrying out of the God-ordained way to meet and to serve is to exercise the New Testament priesthood of the gospel by helping people to be saved and baptized. This is to beget new believers. We may help people to be saved and baptized through visiting them in their homes by knocking on their doors. However, we should not be legal about our way. Sometimes we may help them in other ways, such as inviting them to a meeting or simply speaking to them on the street. The second step in carrying out the God-ordained way is to feed the new ones by meeting with them in their homes. These new beginners may be those who have been saved and baptized among us, or they may be other new believers whom we have met. The third step is to perfect the new believers in group meetings. After feeding the new ones for a short time, we should bring them together to form a group meeting, not just for feeding but for perfecting. This meeting is the main part of the church life, and it should include fellowship, intercession, care, shepherding, teaching, perfecting, and all the other items of the church life. The fourth step in the God-ordained way is to prophesy in the larger church meetings. These four steps for carrying out the God-ordained way to meet and to serve should not merely be something we learn. They should be our daily walk. We should take this way and walk in this way.

THE WAY TO HAVE A GROUP MEETING

There are many ways to have a group meeting. When the attendants of the meeting come together, they may spontaneously begin to sing and pray. Then one brother may tell the others that one of the new sisters has become ill, and the group may pray for her. There are many things about which we can fellowship in the meeting. Someone may ask about a brother's job situation, and the group may again pray and seek the Lord's leading in caring for him and his family. One who is exercising to care for a group meeting will be able to know when one person has been speaking for too long about a particular matter. Then he can introduce something else into the meeting. He may offer a prayer, and his prayer will change the atmosphere of the meeting and bring it into another stage.

The teaching in the group meetings should be carried out not by a particular person but by all the attendants in that meeting. During the group meeting, a brother may raise a question concerning a point from the Bible. Everyone in the group can teach the others by saying something in answer to that question. Even those who have been saved for a very short time have something to speak and can offer it in the meeting. Likewise, there are often some attendants who are able to speak something deeper in answer to the questions, and some who are able to give a concluding word. Everyone has a small portion, and when everyone presents what he has, all the portions are added together to make a good teaching. Everyone can ask a question, everyone can answer, and everyone can teach. Whatever is spoken in the group meeting is heard by all the attendants, and everyone receives the help. This is the way to teach the saints in a group meeting. If the saints attend this kind of group meeting week after week for two or three years, they will be perfected.

If we practice having group meetings, we will learn the proper way to carry them out. The best way to learn is to practice. The more we practice, the more we learn. We should not say that we do not know how to cook. We should simply buy some groceries, put them into water, and place them on a stove. Then we will learn to cook. If we would practice having group meetings for several months, we will know how to meet, and we will receive the benefit. When we have learned the proper way to have group meetings, they will become indispensable.

The group meetings comprise eighty percent of the church life if we practice them properly. However, we may not know how to have group meetings in life, in spirit, and according to everyone's current situation and need. This is because we have been accustomed to having meetings in a traditional, formal, ritualistic way. In the old way of meeting, we could meet for some years and still not know the other attendants in the meeting. There might be no contact, care, or shepherding among the members. In a church with several hundred newly baptized believers, it would be impossible to have enough elders to care for them all. If such a church meets in the old way, the number of new ones will be impressive, but there will be little content of reality. However, if this church meets in a proper way, the several hundred members will be formed into groups of eight to fifteen persons. Each group will care for the persons in that group. The members of the group will come to know one another very well, and the entire church will be under a daily, mutual care. This mutual care is carried out in many ways in the group meetings.

BEING RELEASED, LIVING, AND FRESH

For the sake of the group meetings, we must always be released, living, and fresh. We must not be under any bondage. Almost everyone on earth is in some kind of "shackle." Every day we may be shackled. We may not be free persons, persons who are released, living, and fresh. As a result, we are in debt to the Lord. We owe Him praises, songs, speakings, and testimonies. If we are released persons who are living and fresh, the Spirit within us has the full freedom to move. However, many times when we come together, it seems as if we do not have the Spirit. Instead, we wait on the Spirit to come and release us. The Bible tells us that we have a human spirit (Job. 32:8; Zech. 12:1) and the divine Spirit (Rom. 8:9, 11, 16). To wait for something that we already have is wrong. We have the divine Spirit in our human spirit, so we should exercise our mingled spirit. It does not matter whether or not we feel our spirit. We do not need to feel our spirit; we only need to use it.

We Christians are the people of a speaking God. In the New Testament, God speaks in the principle of incarnation. He does not speak only by Himself; He speaks through our speaking. If we speak, He speaks in our speaking. If we do not speak, we stop His speaking. Therefore, we must exercise our spirit whenever we come together. When we turn on a light switch, the electricity operates. In the same way, when we exercise our spirit by crying, "O Lord Jesus!" we have the sensation that the Holy Spirit is moving within us. This is because as Christians we have a regenerated, enlivened, and strengthened human spirit that has been mingled with the divine Spirit. The Spirit never leaves our spirit. He remains in our spirit and is mingled with it at all times. Therefore, we are able to exercise our spirit at any time and in any place. The problem is that many times we do not exercise our spirit. Because we do not move, the Spirit has no way to move. He becomes shackled by us. When we exercise our spirit to testify in the meetings, we shake off the shackles.

A number of years ago, when I would give messages, I often would not use an outline for my speaking. When it was time to speak, I would simply walk up to the podium. I did not have any verses prepared, but when it was time for the Scripture reading, the verses I needed for my message would come to me. Likewise, when I would begin to speak, the message itself would come to me. If we exercise our spirit, the Spirit within us rises up, because the Spirit is one with our spirit. No one can separate the two. The Spirit has been put into our spirit to be the very essence of our spiritual being. Thus, we do not need to wait for the Spirit, because the Spirit is our very essence. We simply need to use our mingled spirit.

We need to be trained and even disciplined to meet in a released, living, and fresh way. Many times our meetings are dead, cold, old, poor, and low because we are still shackled. For this reason it is difficult to have group meetings. The group meetings need at least one person who is released, living, fresh, and unshackled. If such a person meets with a group for two or three weeks, the entire group will be affected by him. All the attendants in that group meeting will become the same as he is. In that group meeting the new believers all will be released, living, and refreshed because from the day they first became Christians they participated in released, living, and refreshing meetings. They will not know any other way to meet. Without shouting, praising, and saying, "O Lord! Amen!" they would not consider that they have been to a meeting. However, many of us are not this way. For many years we have been molded to be what we are today, always coming to the meetings in the same way. If this is our habit, it will be very difficult to have proper group meetings.

To have group meetings in the old way is easy. According to the old way, the elders divide the church into several groups and appoint a leader for each group. If they have difficulty finding a leader among all the attendants in a certain group, they may either combine groups or appoint a brother from a different area to join that group. However, even these leaders may be examples of deadness to the new ones. They may call a hymn in a dead way and lead the reading of some lessons in a dead way. Group meetings conducted in this way are meetings with no spirit, no release, no livingness, and no freshness.

We must be released, living, and refreshed persons. Then we should forget about all formality and ritual and exercise our spirit to testify, sing, praise, shout, speak, pray for others, and care for others. The group meetings depend on our daily living. We must live a life that is released, living, and refreshing, and we need to keep a constant fellowship with the Lord all day long. We must be persons living in the Lord's presence and spending time daily with the Lord to study His Word. In this way we will spontaneously have an accumulation of Christ in our daily life. This accumulation will become our spiritual riches, our spiritual "capital," to "spend" in the meetings. We will be released, living, and refreshing, and we will have the riches of Christ as a deposit. Then, when we come to the group meetings, we will be released. We will speak, and we will have a content of Christ with which to speak. If we are such persons, we will be very "contagious" and will "infect" others. What we do in the meetings will not be a performance. It will be the issue of what we are and the spontaneous way we live and behave. We will be able to shout, praise, sing, and speak in a living way. This is the way to have the proper church life.

If we are such living persons, it will be easy for us to release sinners. We may not be released but may be shackled when we go to knock on people's doors. If this is the case, the people may open their doors to us, but what we say will not be releasing. What comes out of our minds will not release people; rather, it will bind them. However, if we are released persons, we can speak the same words, but the spirit in our speaking will be different. When we speak, our word will release people and it will stir up the interest of those to whom we speak. Today many Christians are seeking spiritual power from on high. However, the real power is in our being released persons. A released, living, and refreshing Christian lives in the spirit, and when he uses his spirit, the Holy Spirit comes out. It is easy for such persons to help people be saved and, after they are saved, to spend time with them to feed them. We must all learn to live such a life and be such persons. If we all become such persons, after a short time the entire church will be revived. This kind of revival will be a real, constant, and continuous revival.

Chapter Five

BEARING FRUIT AND CARING FOR THE NEW BELIEVERS

To go on in the Lord's new way, the God-ordained way to meet and to serve, requires much study. We have had much speaking and teaching concerning the new way, and we have discovered many crucial points related to it. This speaking has been printed in messages and is available to read. Although we have been going on steadily in the new way, our going on has been too slow. We now need to rise up to practice the new way.

CONTACTING PEOPLE FOR THE PREACHING OF THE GOSPEL

The first step in the Lord's new way is to contact people to bring them the gospel of the kingdom, which is the gospel of Christ. In order to contact people for the gospel, we should not merely stay home to pray for them and invite them to come to us. We have learned that this is not adequate. One effective and time-saving way to contact others for the gospel is to use the telephone. This way has been used very much by the marketing industry. Some saints have begun to call people to make appointments to share the gospel with them. This is an improved way to contact others. Some people may not be willing to make an appointment, but due to the telephone calls, they may come to the Lord's Day morning meeting. One church has begun to keep a guest book to record many details concerning each new one who comes to the meetings. Once a new one comes to the meeting, the saints will write them a letter or visit them. We should not trust that the new ones will contact us. Rather, we must exercise to contact them by many means.

There are many ways to visit people, and we still need more learning in this matter. If we are going to gain people, we must contact them. If a business receives only three replies for every one hundred brochures they mail out, they will recover their expenses. Likewise, for us to gain even one person out of five hundred contacts would be profitable and worthwhile. We do not expect a large increase. We only expect that each member in the Lord's recovery will gain one person yearly. Through this onefold increase we will double our number every year. However, according to our study of church history, it is hard to find a church that has had even a thirty percent annual increase.

BEARING FRUIT

It is not good to be barren and unfruitful. The biggest commission from the Lord to His disciples is to go and disciple all the nations (Matt. 28:19), and the greatest charge to the New Testament believers is to bear fruit (John 15:4-8), to get people saved. It is not right to be a Christian for many years, and yet be without fruit. We should not take any excuse for not bearing fruit.

It is a joy to have some dear ones under our care who are younger or weaker than we are. The people in the world seek amusements to make them joyful. Our joy is Christ, but we cannot enjoy Christ well without fruit-bearing. Without fruit-bearing our enjoyment of Christ is in vain. To have children physically is a joy, but in the eyes of God spiritual children are much more precious than physical children. If we have two or three spiritual children under our care, they will be our comfort, strengthening, encouragement, and daily joy year-round, and we will feel that we know the meaning of our Christian life better. On the other hand, if we do not have anyone under our spiritual care, we may wonder what the purpose of being a Christian is, and the enjoyment of Christ will eventually lose its taste.

We all have to pray, saying, "Lord, I hate barrenness, and I love to bear fruit. If I cannot have two or three of Your children to be my children, I will not be happy. Year after year I always want two or three younger Christians under my care." We must endeavor to reach the goal of fruit-bearing. Then our Christian life will be meaningful, and our enjoyment of Christ will always be fresh. Whether or not the enjoyment of Christ is fresh to us depends on fruit-bearing as the result, the issue, of our enjoyment of Christ. To abide in Christ is the main charge in John 15 (v. 4a), but this charge is for another charge—to bear fruit (vv. 4b-8). Abiding is for fruit-bearing. It is impossible for a branch to abide in the vine and enjoy all the riches and life juice from the root of the vine without bearing fruit. The thought that we can abide in Christ without bearing fruit is a self-deceit from the source of Satan. We must condemn this thought. We cannot promote the enjoyment of Christ without fruit-bearing. We should not be satisfied with the enjoyment of Christ in vain. The enjoyment of Christ must have an issue. This issue is not merely the growth of the branch but fruit-bearing. We must have fruit-bearing, and we must have children to care for. In John 15:16 the Lord said, "I appointed you that you should go forth and bear fruit, and that your fruit should remain." To go forth is to contact people, and to have our fruit remain is by taking care of the young ones. Without our caring for the young ones, our fruit cannot remain.

FRUIT-BEARING CAUSING US TO REALIZE OUR SHORTAGE

If we rise up to bear fruit and care for the young ones, we will realize our shortage. We will realize that we do not have enough growth in the divine life. To be a Christian we need to grow, but we may have been in the Lord and in the church for many years without the proper growth in life. We may have been content merely to come to the meetings without any desperation for the growth in life. We would be bothered if our child had no growth after several years, Likewise, we all have to be bothered about our lack of growth in life. The way some dear saints speak and consider the things concerning the church indicates that they are not only childish but also babyish. They have too little growth in life. The reason we may lack the growth in life but still be content is that we do not care for fruit-bearing and taking care of the young ones. Once we rise up to bear fruit and care for spiritual children, we will discover that we need the growth in life.

OUR NEED FOR THE GROWTH IN LIFE AND SKILL IN CONTACTING PEOPLE

Many saints have been spiritually disabled by the lack of growth in life and the shortage of skill. On the one hand, we may lack the growth in life. On the other hand, even if we go to contact people, we may not have the skill to converse with them. To speak to people properly requires much learning and coaching. Without being taught by a "coach," we will not be able to "play ball." We will just "play" in the natural way, which is not effective. We need to be coached in every aspect of speaking to people. After being coached for a short time, we will be able to speak very skillfully.

It is not right to be fruitless, but to bear fruit requires skill. Therefore, there is the need of much learning. We must endeavor to learn. We all can use our leisure time to learn something for the Lord. Daily we may need eight hours for sleeping and eight hours for working. This leaves some leisure time. Worldly leisure leads us into sin, but using our leisure time for spiritual matters leads us into fellowship with the Lord. Using our leisure time in this way will benefit us, our family, our relatives, and society.

We must learn how to contact people, how to reach people, and how to converse with people. In the past we preached the gospel in a casual way. We simply invited people to a gospel meeting every several months. We did not need to learn to speak or to preach. A good speaker took care of the preaching in the meeting. This idle way of letting others serve the Lord for us offends the Lord and offends the principle of the Body of Christ. The church is the Body of Christ, and just as every part of our body functions, all the members of the Body of Christ function. Simply to invite people to a meeting is not adequate.

We cannot expect that there will be many excellent speakers among us. It may even be that in a certain local church there are no good speakers. However, that church must still do something to bear fruit. Not everyone can be a good cook, but everyone can cook something. No family can survive simply by inviting good cooks to cook for them. Such a family will eventually starve. Everyone can cook. After cooking for a certain time, we will learn to cook well. If we cannot cook well, it is because we have not practiced. To depend upon a great evangelist for fruit-bearing is wrong. There are not many big evangelists among us, and those who may be such persons should restrict their functioning in order to let all the saints exercise their function. It is not good for a shoulder to function in a way which annuls the function of the other members. The annulling of the functions of the members is a paralysis in the Body of Christ. We have to keep every part of the Body active and functioning. Then the Body will be healthy.

SETTLING OUR ACCOUNT WITH THE LORD

We should be bothered about our shortage of increase. If we are not bothered today, one day we may be troubled by the Lord Jesus. This is a serious matter. When we go to see Him, He will ask us about our fruit. According to the parable in Matthew 25:14-30, the Lord has delivered His talents to us, and one day He will come and settle accounts with us. In this parable, the one with five talents and the one with two talents gave an account of what they had done, and they received a reward. The one with one talent, however, received a punishment. One day we will have to give the Lord an account. Whether we will receive a reward or a punishment depends upon what we do in this age. To be a Christian is not a small matter. Much preparation is needed for us to meet the Lord. We must go out to gain people, telling the Lord, "You gave me one talent. Now I would make another talent for a profit."

We have to rise up. We have no choice but to be Christians. Therefore, we must be normal Christians, not abnormal and disobedient. In society, if a person does not get an education, he will cause himself to suffer. He has to study and make good grades. Then he will be a better person and will live a better life. In the same way, we must rise up to learn something related to fruit-bearing. When we do so, we will discover that we need the growth in life, and we will grow. By this, our prayer will change. Previously, we might have only known how to pray in an idle way. We did not mean business in our prayer. However, when we rise up to mean business with the Lord, we will pray desperately with much meaning. We may even fast, not according to a teaching, but according to an inner compelling.

OUR NEED OF LEARNING FOR THE GROUP MEETINGS

To have the proper group meetings requires much learning. We should not take the easy, natural way to meet, in which several people come together, sing a hymn, pray, and testify in a natural way. We must pick up the skill of fellowshipping and learn how to stir up others to fellowship. As we have pointed out before, in the group meetings we should have fellowship, prayer, care, and shepherding. To speak these four words is easy, but we need to learn how to practice these things organically in a living way and how to stir up others to cooperate to practice them with us in the meetings. I believe that in the churches there will be small groups full of organic fellowship, organic intercession, organic care for one another, and organic shepherding. That will be very enjoyable and a great encouragement to all the believers. Everyone enjoys having a free talk with their friends. If we have a pleasant free talk, everyone will enjoy taking part in it. The group meetings are a few people coming together to have such a pleasant talk. Coming together in this way makes everybody happy. Eventually everyone in the group will know everyone else. This kind of meeting is a joy. However, we have to learn how to have such a meeting. We have spoken sufficiently on this subject. Our need today is on the side of practice.

To come together in the small groups is also to come together to teach and to be taught. Without teaching we can never carry out the central goal of the group meeting, which is to perfect the saints unto the work of the ministry, unto the building up of the Body of Christ (Eph. 4:12). If we do not know how to teach and receive teaching, we cannot attain to the goal of the group meeting, and our meetings will be too low.

In the practice of the new way, to teach is not merely to open the Bible or a particular book to point out certain truths. This is too legal, dead, and vain. To teach in the new way is mostly to answer practical questions. We should let all the attendants of a group meeting know that everyone is free to raise any kind of question. A new one in the meeting may raise a question concerning the origin of the Bible. The attendants in the meeting must supply some answers, and in order to do this, they must have some learning. For this reason we have published many books, including one which tells us where the Bible came from and how it was composed (see Lesson One in *Truth Lessons—Level One,* volume 1, published by Living Stream Ministry). The books that we have published are real and practical and meet our needs. We should spend our leisure time to read them. By doing so we will accumulate a good store and a rich deposit of the proper spiritual knowledge. Then we will be equipped to attend the group meetings. When any question is raised, we will have something to answer. In our answering of questions, there may even be new light and new discoveries from the Bible.

All the saints should be equipped. In this regard, we hope that none of the saints in the Lord's recovery will take the way of traditional Christianity. Every saint must be knowledgeable. Everyone must be able to teach, and everyone must know what to do in the small group meetings. We must render care to others, but if we do not have the growth in life and are not knowledgeable concerning spiritual things, the things of God in His economy, we will not be able to care for the younger ones. In order to attend the group meetings and take care of the younger ones, we have to endeavor to become qualified, perfected, and equipped. Endeavoring to be equipped in this way is a lifelong matter. We should not stop learning. Rather, because we mean business with the Lord, we should be desperate to learn.

No one is too old to bear fruit and take care of the new ones. The older saints among us can at least pray and care for the older ones among their relatives, neighbors, and friends.

We need to have two or three younger ones under our care constantly. We should pray for them and take care of all their needs, including their physical needs. There are many ways that we can care for the saints. As we care for the saints, the Body of Christ will be cared for and spontaneously built up. Our care for others should not be in the way of traditional Christianity, in which a meeting is established with a gifted one as the speaker. This kind of care is not genuine. If our care for others is like this, we will not have a good report when we go to the Lord to give an account to Him. At that time He will not listen to our excuses. Rather, He may ask whether or not we heard or read these messages concerning fruit-bearing. To hear these messages may be a profit to us. However, to hear these messages places us under an obligation. Now that the Lord has shown us the God-ordained way, we have no excuse. We have to bear fruit and take care of the young ones. This is a serious matter, and this is related to God's economy. If we all do our part in fruit-bearing, God's economy will be fulfilled.

CHAPTER SIX

THE PRACTICE AND GOAL OF THE GROUP MEETINGS

Scripture Reading: Heb. 10:24-25

FELLOWSHIP, INTERCESSION, MUTUAL CARE, AND SHEPHERDING IN THE GROUP MEETINGS

According to our experience and learning and based upon the clear revelation in the New Testament, the proper group meetings should consist of two sections. The first section should include fellowship, intercession, mutual care, and shepherding, and the second section should carry out the perfecting of the saints through teaching. In the first section of the group meeting, the attendants should fellowship concerning each person's present spiritual condition and practical environment. This fellowship should not be by only one or two persons. All the attendants should make their situations known to the others in each meeting. If a brother has become spiritually weak and is bothered by something, he should come to the group meeting and open himself to the other brothers and sisters. To open in this way is to be honest and faithful and to confront the enemy's attack. In the group meetings we should fellowship about the things that concern our present situation. If we have no problems or needs of our own but know of the needs of others, we may fellowship something about their up-to-date situation. This may spontaneously burden some of the saints to pray for that situation.

The group meeting is eighty percent of the church life, and the church life is a life in the Body. In our physical body, it is impossible for a problem in one member to be hidden from all the other members. The circulation of life in our body carries the feeling in one member to all the members. Thus, we should not hide our problems from the other members in the church life. However, in the past we have often tried to hide our troubles from each other. We might have spoken about the world situation, but purposely concealed our own situation from the saints. This kind of practice has annulled the proper church life. When we acted in this way, we did not function as the members of the organic Body of Christ. Rather, we behaved as the members of a civic club. For the practice of the group meetings, we must first overcome this to have a real, genuine, practical, and thorough fellowship concerning each person's current spiritual condition and practical situation. A proper group meeting does not depend on singing and praying in a formal, religious way. It depends on this kind of fellowship.

After fellowshipping about each other's situations, the attendants in the meeting will spontaneously be stirred up to intercede, to pray, for one another. This prayer will not be formal or like a theatrical performance, but will be sincere and practical. After the fellowship and prayer, the attendants in the group meeting should extend their loving concern for one another in the exercise of a definite and practical care. After becoming aware of a brother's practical situation, some saints in the meeting may consider whether the brother is in need of financial help or some other practical care. Then, after caring for a brother in this way, some may go to visit him. This is the practice of the practical shepherding.

I would say that this principle regarding the practice of the group meetings is "scientific." As such, it cannot be changed. Everything in this universe is governed by a God-ordained law, a spontaneous principle. In order for the church to be fully built up, we must have proper group meetings, and for the group meetings in the practical church life, there is the need of fellowship, intercession, care, and shepherding. In this way, every member of the church, regardless of how large that church may be, will be taken care of. The way to care for every member of the church is by the proper group meetings.

Based on Hebrews 10:24-25, I believe that in the apostles' time the church practiced the group meetings in this way. These verses say, "And let us consider one another for inciting to love and good works, not forsaking the assembling of ourselves together, as the custom with some is, but exhorting one another, and so much the more as you see the day drawing near." In these verses there are three crucial words: *consider, incite,* and *exhort.* Verse 24 charges us to consider one another. The word *consider* is very meaningful. To consider one another implies to remember, to have a sincere, loving concern for one another. It implies that the saints are in our heart. This verse goes on to say that we should incite one another to love and good works. *Good works* here refers to giving something to others freely or doing something freely for others. To give a financial gift or to care for a sick brother is a good work. There is the need for many such good works in the Body. We need to incite one another unto love and unto this kind of good work. Verse 25 also says that we are to exhort one another. Considering one another, inciting one another, and exhorting one another cannot be accomplished in the big meetings. They can be carried out only in the small group meetings.

THE PERFECTING OF THE SAINTS THROUGH TEACHING IN MUTUALITY

The fellowship, intercession, care, and shepherding in the first section of the group meeting are the beginning and the base of the group meetings. Without such a base, we cannot have effective group meetings. However, these items in the first section of the group meeting cannot fulfill the purpose of the group meeting or reach its goal. The purpose and goal of the group meetings is the perfecting of the saints through teaching in mutuality.

The way to have the proper teaching in a group meeting is not by waiting for an assigned teacher to speak. Rather, the best way is to teach by asking questions. There are no assigned teachers in the group meetings; all the attendants are teachers. Although the sisters should not teach with authority by defining and deciding the meaning of doctrines concerning divine truth (1 Tim. 2:12), they can still teach in the way of exhortation. A sister can say, "Brothers and sisters, we all need to be sanctified from the world unto God by the holy word." Then another sister may ask what sanctification is, and a brother can give a defining word on the meaning of sanctification. He may say, "To be sanctified is to be separated from the world." Another may say, "Sanctification is to be made holy unto God in our position." A third one may say, "Sanctification is to be made holy unto God also in our disposition." A fourth may say, "Formerly, we were mixed with the world, but sanctification separates us from that situation unto God. Then, this sanctification continues by separating us from the negative things in our disposition. This is equivalent to transformation." In this way every attendant in the group meeting can teach, regardless of how little he can do. Each answer to the questions raised in a group meeting becomes part of the teaching in that meeting.

The goal of the group meeting is to perfect the saints. Without teaching, it is impossible to reach this goal. In a group meeting, the best way to teach is to ask. Even if we have a burden to teach and exhort others concerning a particular matter, we should not release our burden directly. Rather, we should turn our teaching into a question. Once we ask a question, all the attendants in the meeting will have the obligation to say something, and they will all become teachers. The best way to learn something thoroughly is to teach it. Often we can learn more by teaching than by listening.

We should not think that we know everything there is to know about any teaching in the Bible. In the matter of knowing, there is no limit. Sometimes one who has been saved for only a short time will speak something that is new to the other members. The more attendants there are in a group meeting, the more knowledge there is. However, the knowledge that is within the attendants should be released. Meeting in the old, traditional way did not give the saints the way to release what was within them, but by our meeting in the new way, everything that is in the saints can be released.

The group meetings are our meetings. Therefore, all the attendants in a group meeting must take care of the meeting. In our natural being and in the traditional practice of Christianity there is not the thought that every member must care for the meetings, but in the new way this thought must be sown into us. We should not go to the meetings without a sense of obligation. If each person does not take care of the meetings, the meetings will be poor. Each person in the meeting must be both a teacher and a learner.

OUR NEED FOR LEARNING AND THE EXPERIENCE OF LIFE

In order to take care of a group meeting and answer the questions asked by the new ones, we need to learn a great deal. We must know the truth, the experience of life, and the current situation of the saints and the Lord's move. Without such learning, we are not qualified to care for the saints by answering their questions. On the one hand, to teach in the group meeting is easy. All the attendants need only to express something according to their experience. Even if one has been a Christian for only one week, he will have had some experience and will have something to say. On the other hand, it is not easy to be effective in our carrying out of the purpose and goal of the group meetings. To take care of a group meeting requires that we have much ability and a large capacity. We all have an ability, a skill, related to the group meetings. However, our ability has a capacity, a limit. The more we function according to our ability, the more our capacity will be increased. We all need much learning, and we need to be trained. We need to study the Bible and read the proper spiritual books. We also need to use our time wisely to study other positive matters, such as humanity, history, and foreign languages. This will equip us and enable us and will enlarge our capacity.

To take care of the group meetings, we need to have a large capacity that is full of ability. To be the proper Christians that God desires for the carrying out of His New Testament economy in this age requires that we mean business with Him. If we are not such capable persons, the Lord will not have the way to return, because He will not be able to build up His organic Body. However, the Lord's sovereignty is adequate. Eventually He will have the opportunity to carry out His New Testament economy, and the way in which He will do this is the new way that He is unveiling to us in these days. Today we are pioneering the new way, and eventually many others will take this way also.

We must learn to know the truth, and we must learn to know the genuine experience of life. We need the foundation of life, the Spirit, the apostles' teaching, the subjective experience of the cross, and resurrection. I have no desire to pass on to the saints mere spiritual or biblical knowledge. My intention is to bring all the saints into the full realization of the experience of life. In life we must experience the cross of Christ subjectively, and we must also experience resurrection, which in reality is the pneumatic Christ. We must experience these things in our daily life. When we are about to exchange words with our spouse or with the brothers, we must first ask ourselves, "Am I doing this under the cross? Is this in resurrection?" This is the experience of life.

The first two lines of *Hymns,* #631, say,

> If I'd know Christ's risen power,
> I must ever love the Cross.

If we do not live a life under the cross and in the resurrection of Christ, whatever we can do and whatever we would do will mean nothing. We need to learn many things in order to be adequately equipped. We also need to learn to serve the Lord and work for Him under the cross and in resurrection. We must learn the lesson of life in the Spirit; that is, in doing anything we need to consider how much we are under the cross and how much we are in resurrection.

CHAPTER SEVEN

TEACHING IN THE GROUP MEETINGS

THE FELLOWSHIP IN THE GROUP MEETINGS

The purpose and goal of the group meetings is the perfecting of the saints through teaching in mutuality, and the best way to carry out the teaching is by asking and answering the proper questions. However, it is better to begin the group meetings with fellowship, intercession, care, and shepherding; these constitute the foundation of the group meetings. In order to build up anything, there is the need to first lay a foundation. In order to teach one another, there is the need for us first to know each other. When people know each other, there is a pleasant feeling between them. Their hearts are opened and softened. If someone who does not know the brothers and sisters is invited to speak to them, they may receive what he speaks, but his word will not be intimate or very effective. The saints will not feel at home with the speaker. Such a lack of intimacy will frustrate the mutual speaking and mutual understanding in the meeting. Thus, every time we come together to have a group meeting, we must warm each other up and become intimately acquainted again. Then the saints will be prepared to be taught by one another. They will be open, and there will be no uneasy feeling and no frustration to the mutual speaking and mutual understanding. This is why such a foundation is needed in every group meeting.

In the group meetings we should not neglect the fellowship regarding the personal situation of the saints; however, neither should we overemphasize this fellowship. An overemphasizing of the fellowship will damage the meeting. When we come to the group meetings, we must open ourselves and make ourselves known to one another, but in doing so there is the danger of going too far. If we go too far in our fellowship, we will bring in looseness. When we open ourselves, we should not do so without restraint. We must learn the proper way to open ourselves and not use too great a part of the meeting for this purpose. Since we are only one of many persons in the meeting, we should control ourselves and use only a brief time for our speaking concerning ourselves.

ASKING PROFITABLE QUESTIONS IN THE GROUP MEETINGS

In asking questions in the group meetings, we need to consider whether the subject of our questions is profitable to all the saints. We should avoid asking questions that are peculiar. If a peculiar question is asked in a group meeting—for example, someone may ask when mankind began to have different colors of skin—we should not answer it, but should pray and seek for a proper way to redirect the speaking to a more profitable line. There are many things that we do not understand, even concerning ourselves. Deuteronomy 29:29 says, "The secret things belong unto the Lord our God." The Lord keeps many things hidden from us and permits us to know only the things that are profitable for us. Our questions should concern profitable matters, such as the truths in Romans 8. The truths in this chapter are deep and, to some extent, mysterious, but they are logical and very profitable.

The old way of meeting kept everyone in a deadened and regulated condition; for the most part, this prevented peculiar things from taking place in the meetings. For the group meetings in the new way, however, we should be released. We should be free and not bound. When a group meeting becomes prevailing, everyone in it will be free, but this may open the door for certain peculiar things to come in. Thus, in the group meetings we should not be bound, but neither should we be free without limitation.

OUR NEED FOR MUCH LEARNING

Our Need to Read the Bible

The most valuable and difficult aspect of the group meetings is the teaching through the raising and answering of questions. When we answer questions in the group meetings, we need to consider them very much and answer with the best utterance and in the most excelling way. Paul said, "Seek that you may excel for the building up of the church" (1 Cor. 14:12, lit.). We must seek the excelling gift, so that whatever we have may excel for the building up of the church. Therefore, we all need to learn the truth, and for this we all must study the Bible. When Brother Nee was a student, he determined that he would read through the New Testament every week for a year. Wherever he went he carried a New Testament and would read a small portion at a time. He later said that that year of reading the New Testament was the most profitable time in his life in knowing the Bible.

In expounding any book of the Bible, even a book such as Daniel, which contains many prophecies, my main burden is to speak concerning Christ and His salvation and concerning our enjoyment of Christ and His salvation. However, it is difficult to see these matters in a book without reading it a number of times and studying it thoroughly. We all need the thorough and continual study of the Word year after year. Even if we have a certain understanding of a book of the Bible, we should still read it again and again. Many of us have a good understanding of the book of Romans, but if we would read it again once a week for three weeks, our understanding of it would become solid and crystal clear. It is good to read the entire Bible once a year. At least we can finish the New Testament once a year and read through the Old Testament every two or three years. To read the New Testament once a year and the Old Testament once every three years requires that we read only one chapter from the New Testament and one from the Old Testament each day. In order to read through the Bible in this way, we need to read it quickly, taking only a few minutes to read each chapter. If we carry a pocket-sized Bible, we can take a few minutes of our lunch time to finish one or more chapters. In this kind of quick reading, we do not need to ponder, meditate, or dwell on the verses as we do in morning watch. If during our quick reading we do not understand certain portions of the Word, we do not need to be concerned; we may understand these portions when we read them the second time, or we may understand them after additional readings.

Our Need of Reference Books and the Proper Spiritual Writings

Reading through the Word of God in this way does not mean that we should read without help from reference books. Without the proper references it is difficult to understand the Bible. We cannot understand the Bible through our own thought alone. Often we may find a word that we do not understand properly. Instead of relying on our own consideration in deciding on the correct denotation of the word, we should consult the proper reference books.

Colossians 3:16 says, "Let the word of Christ dwell in you richly." We need to let the word of Christ, the Bible, dwell in us richly. At the same time we should also read the proper spiritual writings. In the Lord's recovery there are many worthwhile publications. A number of good books have been written by other writers also over the past nineteen centuries. Brother Nee took the lead to read many of these books and laid a good foundation for us in knowing the best ones. After Brother Nee, we continued to read the proper writings, and we now have an accurate understanding concerning which books are the most profitable.

To be a proper person in society, we must be educated for many years. We need to study for approximately seventeen years in order to receive a bachelor's degree. To receive one or more advanced degrees requires two to six more years of study. This is not a waste of our time. If we do not study for the required number of years, our education will be inadequate. It is the same in the spiritual life. My intention in setting up the full-time training is not to teach people a set of beliefs and practices as the seminaries of the denominations do; it is to help the saints to know life and to have the proper knowledge of the holy Word. In order to have the proper knowledge, we must read the Bible, the publications in the Lord's recovery, and the proper spiritual writings of others. By doing so we will be helped, built up, and equipped not only in life but also in truth. Then our presence in the group meetings will be a great benefit.

Answering Questions according to Our Learning

During the teaching in a group meeting, someone may ask an important question, such as, "What is the most crucial point in the Bible?" We should all pay our full attention to a question of this nature and answer it in an all-inclusive way. One brother may say, "The entire Bible unveils to us that the Triune God, after being processed, has become life to the tripartite man for the fulfillment of His eternal economy concerning the church." This answer covers the entire Bible. It requires much explanation, so a second brother can explain how the Triune God was processed, a third can speak regarding what it means for God to become life to man, and a fourth can give a word about the tripartite man. Then a fifth brother can speak something concerning God's eternal economy, a sixth can speak concerning the church as the Body of the One who fills all in all, and a seventh can speak a word concerning the fulfillment of God's eternal economy. In this way, the first answer can be followed by six or seven teachings. After that, there may be many other smaller portions given as part of such a combined teaching. If the teaching in a group meeting reaches this standard, the church in that locality will be strong and high. To answer a question in this way, however, requires much reading of the Scriptures and of the proper spiritual publications and the receiving of the divine revelations.

Other questions may be asked that restrict the fellowship in the meeting instead of releasing it. For example, in a group meeting a sister may ask what head covering is. This question should not be rejected, but it must be answered in a way that will turn a somewhat "cold" subject such as head covering into a "warm" one. How well we can do this depends on our ability, which comes out of our capacity. If we have studied the Bible and the proper publications, we can turn a "hard" subject into a "soft" one. In answering a question concerning head covering, we should not speak merely about the covering on a sister's head. Rather, we may begin by saying, "Sister, this is a good question, because it touches God's headship." Such a word, spoken in a pleasant tone, will "warm up" the meeting. We can then go on to speak from several angles concerning our being subject to God.

OUR NEED OF PROGRESS AND ADVANCEMENT

Regardless of how much we can do in the group meetings, we will often feel that we are inadequate. This indicates that we all need much learning. In the old way of meeting, we came together year-round with little improvement. The meetings were repetitious and uninteresting, and they were full of oldness and staleness. In the group meetings in the new way, it should not be like this. There should be something new in each meeting. However, we should not depend on all the attendants in the group meetings to produce something new. Out of ten attendants there may be only one or two who can cause the atmosphere to be uplifted and refreshing. We must be this kind of person. For this we need not only the proper knowledge but also the experience and the excelling way to present what we have. This means that we must learn.

I do not like to see the churches always remain the same. We need to progress, and we need to advance. We need to advance in knowledge, and we need to advance in the way in which we present what we have. We should not tell people that we have taken the new way, and yet we ourselves remain the same. Concerning life Paul said, "We also should walk in newness of life" (Rom. 6:4), and concerning service he said, "We should serve as slaves in newness of spirit" (Rom. 7:6).

It is easy to be a Christian in the old, traditional way. In the old way there is little requirement or demand, but in the new way there is a great demand. However, we should not be anxious about this. If we were not able to meet the demand, the Lord would not require it of us. The fact that He requires something of us and charges us to do it indicates that He will also carry it out (1 Thes. 5:24). We have seen the positive results of the new way, but there is still the need for greater improvement.

Chapter Eight

BEARING CHILDREN THROUGH THE GOSPEL IN THE DILIGENT PRACTICE OF THE NEW WAY

Scripture Reading: Luke 14:21-23; 19:13; Rom. 1:14-15; 1 Cor. 9:17, 21-25; Phil. 1:27; Col. 1:27-29

THE PREACHING OF THE GOSPEL IN THE NEW TESTAMENT

In order to emphasize the importance of the preaching of the gospel, the New Testament uses different figures of speech in referring to it. In Luke 14:21-23, which contains several crucial points regarding the gospel, the Lord used the figure of an invitation to a feast. These verses say, "And the slave came up and reported these things to his lord. Then the master of the house was angry and told his slave, Go out quickly into the streets and lanes of the city, and bring in here the poor and crippled and blind and lame. And the slave said, Lord, what you commanded has been done, and still there is room. And the lord said to the slave, Go out into the roads and hedges and compel them to come in, that my house may be filled." Verse 21 says that the master of the house was angry. The Bible does not often say that our God is angry; thus, it is not a small thing for the Lord to be angry. He is angry because of the vacant seats at His banquet. He has prepared the banquet of the gospel, but not enough people have come.

The master of the house charged his slave to go out quickly to bring others. The word *quickly* is significant. However, almost two thousand years have passed since this word was spoken. The Lord has been angry yet patient for a very long time. The master told his slave to go into the streets and lanes of the city. The front door of people's houses is usually accessible from the streets, whereas the back door often is approached from the lanes. This indicates that we must go to people at their front door, their back door, or in any way that we can. We must do everything we can to gain people. The slave brought in the poor, the crippled, the blind, and the lame, but still there was room at the banquet. Because of this, the master of the house, still angry, sent his slave out again into the roads (the highways) and hedges outside the city to find those who were idle and to compel them to come in, that his house might be filled.

In Luke 19:13 the Lord used the figure of a master and his servants. The master made his servants businessmen and gave them the capital with which to do business. Verse 13 says, "And having called ten of his own slaves, he gave them ten minas, and said to them, Do business until I come." I appreciate the word "Do business until I come." The phrase *until I come* literally means *while I am coming.* While the Lord is on His way to come, we must be on our way to do the business of the gospel.

In Romans 1:14-15 Paul used the figure of a debtor. In these verses Paul said, "I am debtor both to Greeks and to barbarians, both to wise and to foolish. So, as far as depends on me, I am ready to preach the gospel to you also who are in Rome."

First Corinthians 9:17 says, "For if I do this voluntarily, I have a reward; but if not of my own will, I have been entrusted with a stewardship." The word *stewardship* is another figure of speech used in reference to gospel preaching. Every preacher is a steward. Verses 22-25 of the same chapter say, "To the weak I became weak, that I might gain the weak. To all men I have become all things, that I might by all means save some. And I do all things for the sake of the gospel, that I may become a fellow partaker of it. Do you not know that those who run in a racecourse all run, but one receives the prize? So run, that you may lay hold. And everyone who contends exercises self-control in all things; those, therefore, that they may receive a corruptible crown, but we an incorruptible." In these verses Paul used the figure of contending in the Olympics to describe the importance of gospel preaching.

Philippians 1:27 says, "Only conduct yourselves worthily

of the gospel of Christ, that whether coming and seeing you or being absent I may hear the things concerning you, that you stand firm in one spirit, with one soul striving together in the faith of the gospel." We need to conduct ourselves in a way that is worthy of the gospel of Christ. Our conduct must match the gospel. We also must stand firm in one spirit, with one soul striving together, struggling like Olympic athletes, in the faith of the gospel.

Colossians 1:27-28 says, "To whom God willed to make known what are the riches of the glory of this mystery among the nations, which is Christ in you, the hope of glory: whom we announce, warning every man and teaching every man in all wisdom, that we may present every man full-grown in Christ." Again, many different terms are used in these verses to refer to the gospel. The center of the gospel is Christ in us as the hope of glory, but we must bring this news to people and make it known to them. Thus, we must announce Christ as the center of the gospel, warning every man and teaching every man in all wisdom. Here the terms *announce, warn,* and *teach* are used in reference to the gospel. The phrase *in all wisdom* indicates that we must exhaust our wisdom that we may present every man, one by one, full-grown in Christ. Verse 29 says, "For which also I labor, struggling according to His operation which operates in me in power." In this verse the words *labor, struggling,* and *operation* are used in relation to the gospel.

THE LORD IN HIS RECOVERY REQUIRING US AND STIRRING US UP TO PRACTICE THE GOD-ORDAINED WAY

In the past several years many messages have been given regarding the new way, which is actually the God-ordained way to meet and to serve. Through all these messages the God-ordained way has been made very clear to us. At first there was a certain amount of opposition and criticism against the new way, but now there is not much opposition. Almost all the leading ones in the churches in the Lord's recovery are very clear concerning the new way. However, in relation to the practicing of the new way, we can see many "clouds," but we have not yet seen the "rain." The new way has been made clear to us, yet our response has not been quick, adequate, and prevailing.

Many dear saints have a heart to take the new way, but they feel that it is not easy to do so. It is wrong to say that the new way does not work. The new way does work. In a sense, however, it is not easy to take the new way. Christianity has made every believer idle. When a person first enters into Christianity, he may be busy for a short while. Certain denominations require that a new member learn a number of doctrines and pass an examination before he can be baptized. However, after being baptized, a believer may become idle for the rest of his life. All that may be required of such a believer is that he come to the Sunday morning service, leave an offering, and behave properly. By the Lord's mercy and grace, however, there are still a number of seeking ones in Christianity who realize that they are in a situation that is inadequate. This is true especially among those who love to read the Bible. In reading the Bible they discover that they are lacking many spiritual things. They may go to their pastor for help, but many pastors may only quench their seeking, because the pastors themselves have no way to go on.

The situation in the Lord's recovery is not like this. Since the Lord's recovery began in the second century, it has not allowed people to be idle and at peace. The recovery always stirs up people to see what is in the Bible and to seek after it. Throughout the past nineteen centuries, seeking ones have been raised up to discover new truths from the Bible. Many of them put their discoveries into writing, and over the past seventy years we have spent much time and money to find and collect these scattered writings. These discoveries are a part of the Lord's recovery today. As a result, in the Lord's recovery there is much stirring up, and there are many requirements and demands. The Lord's recovery does not allow us to be at ease.

In the past five years we have "dug out" more truths. In particular, we have discovered the New Testament priesthood of the gospel (Rom. 15:16). We have found that the preachers of the gospel should be laboring, energizing, ministering priests of the New Testament. In Romans 15:16

the Greek word for *priest* has a prefix that means *energizing, laboring,* or *ministering.* Such a priesthood of the gospel is a new discovery. Once we see this, we can never be at rest.

The priests in the Old Testament had to offer something every day. They could not cease offering the sacrifices. Their main offerings were the burnt offering, the meal offering, the peace offering, the sin offering, and the trespass offering. Besides these there were many minor offerings. We Christians today, the New Testament believers, also are priests; thus, we must offer something. What we offer should not be merely our praises to the Lord, our material things, or our good conduct. These things are minor offerings. In the New Testament the main offering is saved sinners, who will be transformed to be the members of Christ's Body. In the Old Testament the priests offered the types of the individual Christ; in the New Testament we offer the members of the corporate Christ. For our offering to God we need the saved, sanctified, and transformed members of Christ. The discovery of this truth has changed our understanding of the significance of gospel preaching.

We have also discovered that we must have new ones under our care whom we are feeding. Feeding the new ones is the practice of feeding the lambs (John 21:15) and the practice of a nursing mother feeding her babes (1 Thes. 2:7). Paul said that the apostles were like nursing mothers to the new believers, cherishing and nourishing them that they might grow. Such a practice is absolutely new among us.

I have said that each one of us should have two or three young "lambs" under our care, but we are still short of this kind of feeding. If we do not have at least two or three under our caring hand, then we must "go fishing" to gain some new ones. When I was young, I was desperate to bring new believers to the Lord. If I did not gain some new ones, I could not eat or sleep well. After praying and fasting, I would rise up and go into the streets to speak to people, regardless of what kind of people they were. Where there is a will, there is a way. However, we may not be desperate enough. Consequently, the Lord may be angry with us, because there are still vacant seats at His banquet.

The Lord has also shown us that we must practice the building up of the church through the perfecting of the saints by the apostles, prophets, evangelists, and shepherds and teachers (Eph. 4:11-12). Without exception, every saint must do the same work that the gifted persons do, which is the work of the New Testament ministry, the building up of the Body of Christ. Moreover, we have discovered that there is no way to perfect the saints in big meetings. The perfecting must be carried out in small groups.

We must go to get people saved; we must "get married" in order to bring forth children. After bringing forth children, we need to feed, nourish, and cherish our babes. Then we must perfect them and build them up to speak the word of Christ, to speak Christ, and speak forth Christ to others, that is, to prophesy. If we have such a practice according to the New Testament teaching, no one among us will be idle. However, I am concerned that many of the saints are idle. We may not realize the seriousness of our situation, but one day we will. The Lord said, "Do business until I come." If the Lord would return today and ask us to settle our account with Him, we all would be very serious. The Lord is coming, and we will have to meet Him and give an account to Him (Matt. 25:19; 2 Cor. 5:10). However, today many of the saints are at peace. The new way is a troubling way, not a peacemaking way. We must realize that the new way does not give us rest; rather, it causes us to be busy.

OUR URGENT NEED FOR DILIGENT PRACTICE

Today our urgent need is to practice the new way diligently. The elders, the full-timers, and the co-workers should be the first ones to take the new way. All the elders should take the lead to get new ones saved and to always have two or three new ones under their caring hand. Simply to manage the affairs of the church is not adequate. In a sense, the Lord is not for that. The Lord is for bringing sinners to be saved, regenerated, sanctified, and transformed to be His living members. It is not sufficient merely to have a large number meeting in a local church, because they may be meeting in the way of Christianity, coming together on the Lord's Day merely to constitute a good attendance. We should not shout "Hallelujah!" for merely a good attendance. We must ask whether the attendants are being nourished, sanctified, renewed daily, and transformed. Some may say that they are not able to follow so quickly what I am speaking; they need more time before they can begin to practice this kind of care for new believers. However, we will not be able to say this to the Lord when He comes to settle accounts with us. The Lord has already waited for nearly two thousand years.

The most pleasant thing to the Lord is that those who love Him and seek Him would have two or three new ones under their care. After their children get married, parents always like to see a new child come forth. If a son has been married for three years but does not have a child, his parents may not be happy to visit him. Parents do not want to see their children's rose garden; they want to see grandchildren. If there are two or three grandchildren in a home, the grandparents will want to stay all day to play with them. The Lord desires that two or three new ones be raised up under our caring hand. We may make excuses, saying that it is too hard to get people saved, but the Lord may simply admit that He is a hard man, reaping where He did not sow (Matt. 25:24-26).

Today in every place there is the urgent need of a new beginning. The elders should not wait for the younger ones, and the younger ones should not wait for the elders. We all need to begin to practice this way. I would propose that all the elders, full-timers, and trainees take the lead to get people saved at any cost, forgetting about the other saints and leaving them to the Lord and to themselves.

I do not like fishing because it requires much patience. In fishing, one must spread a net and then draw it in, and there may or may not be fish in it. One may also have to cast a line and wait for a whole day. Fishing is a real test. Likewise, getting people saved is not easy. However, it is also not too difficult. We may visit people by knocking on their doors, or we may call them on the telephone or ask the saints to recommend their relatives to us. We should try our best to find someone to visit for the gospel. In one way or another we need to begin to practice the new way.

After we baptize people, we will treasure them. They will be our treasure and our babies. Then we will have to take care of them, to cherish and nourish them, not just for a few days but for a considerable period of time. Some new ones will need us to care for them for half a year, while others will need our care for a whole year. The goal is to feed them that they may grow. We must practice this.

It is not necessary that we go out to care for others every day. To do this once a week for two or three hours is adequate. On the Lord's Day we should meet for about two hours in the morning to have the Lord's table and to speak the Lord's word to one another. All the saints, new and old, should attend the Lord's Day morning meeting to take the Lord's table and enjoy Him corporately, and to learn to speak for Him. While we are speaking, we will also be listening to others. In this kind of meeting we will hear the word, and spontaneously we will experience much building up. We should try our best to leave the Lord's Day morning free for this. Then one evening a week we should attend the prayer meeting. Do not despise the prayer meeting. By praying only once in the prayer meeting, we may receive more edification than by attending another kind of meeting. We also will receive much enlightenment and exposure for our help. Then one evening a week we should attend a group meeting for fellowship, for our perfecting, and for the perfecting of others. The Lord's Day morning meeting, the prayer meeting, and the group meeting are the three basic church meetings. This still leaves five evenings, two weekend afternoons, and one weekend morning open. Even if we use the entire Saturday for sundry affairs, we will still have five evenings and one afternoon free. We should use one of these six openings to go out for the gospel, either to knock on doors to visit people, to call them on the phone, or to go to the new ones to feed them. This is easy to carry out. It would be even better if we would go out twice a week, one afternoon and one evening, or two evenings a week.

Some may still say that this is difficult to carry out in practice. In the school at which I studied, there were many kinds of sports, but I did not like to play most of them. Many of the sports were difficult for me to play simply because I did not practice. We must practice to go out once or twice a week for the gospel. Even if we do not know how to do it, we should simply do it. We may never have been trained to knock on doors, but we should not care about this. After going out for about one month, we will feel that it is easy. When we see the Lord, we will not be able to excuse ourselves by saying that the new way was too hard. We need to practice.

For many years I have told the saints that we must learn to contact new people, especially after the meetings. However, we have had little practice of this. After a meeting, a sister may go to talk to a sister who is familiar to her. However, in that meeting there may be several new ones who are not being cared for. To talk only with a familiar saint is offending to the Lord and to the church. After a meeting, we should look around to find the new ones. This is pleasing to the Lord and pleasing to the church. We must have the habit of taking care of the new ones. To practice this is not difficult. It is not like learning Hebrew or Greek. We may simply go to a new one, introduce ourselves, and invite him to lunch. This requires that a habit be built up. We do not need to know how to feed someone after baptizing him. We simply need to do it. We should not ask, "With what shall I feed him?" We should simply go to feed him. Most of the new ones appreciate being visited. By doing this we will learn. The first and second time we go we may not know how to feed the new ones, but gradually we will learn. I did not study in a seminary, and I was not taught to speak. I simply practiced, and the more I practiced, the more I learned by doing it.

We should go to get two or three new ones under our care. If we cannot do this, we should come back to pray and fast and then go out again. Our service in the practical affairs of the church may be godly and pious, but it may not be as pleasing to the Lord as going out to knock on doors to gain people. It is better to get sinners saved and baptized and bring them to the church meeting. We have been here for years but we still see the same faces. Even in the group meetings the same eight or ten saints may repeatedly come together, with no new ones. We need some new ones. We need some lambs that we can feed.

About the Author

Witness Lee was born in 1905 in northern China and raised in a Christian family. At age 19 he was fully captured for Christ and immediately consecrated himself to preach the gospel for the rest of his life. Early in his service, he met Watchman Nee, a renowned preacher, teacher, and writer. Witness Lee labored together with Watchman Nee under his direction. In 1934 Watchman Nee entrusted Witness Lee with the responsibility for his publication operation, called the Shanghai Gospel Bookroom.

Prior to the Communist takeover in 1949, Witness Lee was sent by Watchman Nee and his other co-workers to Taiwan to ensure that the things delivered to them by the Lord would not be lost. Watchman Nee instructed Witness Lee to continue the former's publishing operation abroad as the Taiwan Gospel Bookroom, which has been publicly recognized as the publisher of Watchman Nee's works outside China. Witness Lee's work in Taiwan manifested the Lord's abundant blessing. From a mere 350 believers, newly fled from the mainland, the churches in Taiwan grew to 20,000 in five years.

In 1962 Witness Lee felt led of the Lord to come to the United States, and he began to minister in Los Angeles. During his 35 years of service in the U.S., he ministered in weekly meetings and weekend conferences, delivering several thousand spoken messages. Much of his speaking has since been published as over 400 titles. Many of these have been translated into over fourteen languages. He gave his last public conference in February 1997 at the age of 91.

He leaves behind a prolific presentation of the truth in the Bible. His major work, *Life-study of the Bible,* comprises over 25,000 pages of commentary on every book of the Bible from the perspective of the believers' enjoyment and experience of God's divine life in Christ through the Holy Spirit. Witness Lee was the chief editor of a new translation of the New Testament into Chinese called the Recovery Version and directed the translation of the same into English. The Recovery Version also appears in a number of other languages. He provided an extensive body of footnotes, outlines, and spiritual cross references. A radio broadcast of his messages can be heard on Christian radio stations in the United States. In 1965 Witness Lee founded Living Stream Ministry, a non-profit corporation, located in Anaheim, California, which officially presents his and Watchman Nee's ministry.

Witness Lee's ministry emphasizes the experience of Christ as life and the practical oneness of the believers as the Body of Christ. Stressing the importance of attending to both these matters, he led the churches under his care to grow in Christian life and function. He was unbending in his conviction that God's goal is not narrow sectarianism but the Body of Christ. In time, believers began to meet simply as the church in their localities in response to this conviction. In recent years a number of new churches have been raised up in Russia and in many European countries.

Other Books Published By
Living Stream Ministry

Titles by Witness Lee:

Abraham—Called by God	978-0-7363-0359-0
The Experience of Life	978-0-87083-417-2
The Knowledge of Life	978-0-87083-419-6
The Tree of Life	978-0-87083-300-7
The Economy of God	978-0-87083-415-8
The Divine Economy	978-0-87083-268-0
God's New Testament Economy	978-0-87083-199-7
The World Situation and God's Move	978-0-87083-092-1
Christ vs. Religion	978-0-87083-010-5
The All-inclusive Christ	978-0-87083-020-4
Gospel Outlines	978-0-87083-039-6
Character	978-0-87083-322-9
The Secret of Experiencing Christ	978-0-87083-227-7
The Life and Way for the Practice of the Church Life	978-0-87083-785-2
The Basic Revelation in the Holy Scriptures	978-0-87083-105-8
The Crucial Revelation of Life in the Scriptures	978-0-87083-372-4
The Spirit with Our Spirit	978-0-87083-798-2
Christ as the Reality	978-0-87083-047-1
The Central Line of the Divine Revelation	978-0-87083-960-3
The Full Knowledge of the Word of God	978-0-87083-289-5
Watchman Nee—A Seer of the Divine Revelation ...	978-0-87083-625-1

Titles by Watchman Nee:

How to Study the Bible	978-0-7363-0407-8
God's Overcomers	978-0-7363-0433-7
The New Covenant	978-0-7363-0088-9
The Spiritual Man • 3 volumes	978-0-7363-0269-2
Authority and Submission	978-0-7363-0185-5
The Overcoming Life	978-1-57593-817-2
The Glorious Church	978-0-87083-745-6
The Prayer Ministry of the Church	978-0-87083-860-6
The Breaking of the Outer Man and the Release ...	978-1-57593-955-1
The Mystery of Christ	978-1-57593-954-4
The God of Abraham, Isaac, and Jacob	978-0-87083-932-0
The Song of Songs	978-0-87083-872-9
The Gospel of God • 2 volumes	978-1-57593-953-7
The Normal Christian Church Life	978-0-87083-027-3
The Character of the Lord's Worker	978-1-57593-322-1
The Normal Christian Faith	978-0-87083-748-7
Watchman Nee's Testimony	978-0-87083-051-8